A HISTORICAL ALBUM OF

CALIFORNIA

A HISTORICAL ALBUM OF

CALIFORNIA

Charles A. Wills

THE MILLBROOK PRESS, Brookfield, Connecticut

*Front and back cover: "San Francisco." Chromolithograph by M. & N. Hanhart,
from a drawing by Samuel Francis Marryat, London, 1849. Library of Congress.*

*Title page: California Coast Highway along the northern coast. Courtesy of the
California Office of Tourism.*

Library of Congress Cataloguing-in-Publication Data

Wills, Charles.
    A historical album of California / Charles A. Wills.
      p. cm. — (Historical albums)
    Includes bibliographical references and index.
    Summary: A history of California, from its early exploration
and settlement to the state today with its unique status and
influence on America.
    ISBN 1-56294-479-7 (lib. bdg.) ISBN 1-56294-759-1 (pbk.)
    1. California—History—Juvenile literature. 2. California—
Gazetteers—Juvenile literature. I. Title. II. Series.
F861.3.W55 1994
979.4—dc20
                                     93-35015
                                         CIP
                                         AC

 Created in association with Media Projects Incorporated

    C. Carter Smith, *Executive Editor*
    Lelia Wardwell, *Managing Editor*
    Charles A. Wills, *Principal Writer*
    Bernard Schleifer, *Art Director*
    Shelley Latham, *Production Editor*
    Arlene Goldberg, *Cartographer*

    Consultant: Neal Wooley, Miller Junior High School,
San Jose, California

Copyright © 1994 by The Millbrook Press, Inc.

Manufactured in the United States of America

10 9 8 7 6 5 4 3 2

CONTENTS

Introduction

What do you think of when you hear the word "California"? You might think of the snow-capped Sierra Nevada, or the blast-furnace heat of the Death Valley desert, or quiet groves of giant redwood trees. Maybe you picture the hilly streets of San Francisco, the crowded freeways of Los Angeles, the glitter of Hollywood. All of these varied places are part of California.

But California is more than places. California is people. Nearly 30 million people live in California, making it the nation's most populous state. The diversity of California's population is even greater than the variety of its landscape. For more than 150 years, people from all over America—and the world—have come to California to follow their dreams. Some came looking for riches from gold, or oil, or land. Others wanted a better life for themselves and their children. More than anything else, California's history is the story of these people—people who came with a dream and worked hard to make it happen.

Much of California's history is recent. The land was home to a large Native American population for thousands of years, but the first European settlement in California wasn't founded until 1769—just seven years before the United States declared its independence. After periods of Spanish and Mexican rule, California became part of the United States in 1848. Since then, California's growth has been spectacular. The story of California's rise to the first rank—in both population and resources—of all the states is one of the most exciting stories in American history.

PART ONE

THE GOLDEN LAND

California's mountains and valleys have long been a favorite subject of artists and photographers. This landscape painting, by Albert Bierstadt, is titled "Sunset, California Scenery."

A large Native American population lived in California when the first explorers reached the New World. Within a few centuries, almost all of these original inhabitants would be gone—victims of disease, conflict, and the newcomers' hunger for land. The Spanish explored California in the 16th century and founded settlements and missions during the 18th century. In the early 1800s, California came under Mexican rule, but other nations—especially the young United States—also began to take an interest in the region. After a revolt by American settlers, and the U.S. victory in the Mexican War, California became an American territory in 1848. The discovery of gold that same year swelled California's population as fortune hunters poured in by the thousands.

California's Native Americans

No one is sure when the first human beings arrived in California. Archeologists (scientists who study the remains of past societies) have found traces of human settlement dating back about 10,000 years. At sites near the present-day towns of Calico and China Lake, however, archeologists have discovered stone tools that may be more than 200,000 years old.

We do know that as many as 275,000 people lived in California when the first European explorers arrived in the 16th century. These Native Americans—whom the Europeans mistakenly called "Indians"—lived in small groups, or tribes. About 100 tribes lived in California. Some of the larger tribes included the Chumash, Miwok, Pomo, and Shasta Indians, who lived along the Pacific Coast. The Yokut tribe lived in the beautiful Central Valley between the Coast and Sierra Nevada mountain ranges. The blazing deserts of southeastern California were home to the Yuma and Mojave tribes.

California's people spoke an amazing variety of languages—more than twenty primary languages, plus many local variations, called dialects. Often Native Americans from one village couldn't understand the speech of people from another village only a few miles away. Partly because of this diversity, California's Native Americans didn't develop highly organized societies like those found in other parts of North and South America. But language differences didn't make separate tribes enemies, either. Warring between Indian tribes was rare in California.

Most California tribes shared a similar culture and way of life. At the center of Native American life was the village, usually a community of a few hundred people who spoke the same language and were related by blood or marriage. Native American homes were simple structures made of brush and small trees, although houses of redwood planks could be found in northern California. Each village had a *temescal*, or sweat house. Villagers would gather inside the temescal,

This photograph (above, right) shows baskets woven by women of the Pomo tribe. The weave is so tight that these baskets could be used to carry water, and so fine that a magnifying glass is needed to see the individual stitches.

Native American men gather in the village temescal (right). Used for sweat baths and religious ceremonies, the temescal also served as a kind of "town hall," where tribal elders met to make important decisions.

where a fire would be lit. After sweating in the fire's heat, the villagers jumped into a nearby lake or stream. Sweating in the temescal was an important religious ritual in many tribes.

Because much of California has a dry climate with little rainfall, few villages practiced farming. Agriculture was important only to the Mojave and Yuma tribes. They used the water of the Colorado River to grow crops of beans and pumpkins. The rest of California's people gathered and hunted the food they needed. This was easy enough to do. The land was rich with fish, game, and food plants.

Acorns were the most important part of the diet in many villages. After gathering the acorns, the villagers pounded them into flour with stone tools. The acorn flour was soaked in water to wash out its natural acids, then dried in the sun. The process was repeated until the flour was safe to eat. For cooking, flour and water were mixed in a tightly woven basket. Then stones, heated in a fire, were dropped into the basket. The hot stones cooked the mixture into a kind of hot cereal. Berries or nuts might be added for flavor.

Different regions provided different kinds of food. The desert tribes gathered the seed pods of the mesquite plant and dug in the soil for edible roots. Villagers in the mountains ate piñon nuts from pine trees. The rivers of northern California were full of salmon. Along the coast, villagers gathered clams and other shellfish. California's Native Americans hunted with sharpened sticks or with bows and arrows. Sinew—animal tendons—made good bowstrings. Arrows were tipped with obsidian, a substance formed when lava from volcanoes cools and hardens. Because it is easy to shape obsidian, the material was also used for knives and other tools.

The religious life of the California tribes was rich. Religious ideas and rituals differed from tribe to tribe, but most shared a belief in a great being who had created the world, and in many lesser gods and spirits that filled the land. Each village had a shaman, or religious leader. Besides healing the sick, the shaman kept in contact with the world of spirits.

Above all, California's Native Americans lived in close harmony with nature. They depended on the land and the animals that lived on it, and they respected both. The Native Americans never killed an animal unless it was needed for food, and a hunter would thank the animal's spirit for its gift of life.

Piñon nuts and acorn flour were staple foods of Native Americans who lived in the Yosemite Valley (opposite page) and other forested areas of northern California.

An 1876 photograph (below) shows members of the southern branch of the Paiute tribe camped near Mendocino. The Paiutes lived in *wickiups*—huts of sticks and brush fastened to poles made from willow trees.

Early Exploration and Settlement

The first European power to reach California was Spain. Starting with Christopher Columbus's first voyage in 1492, Spain led the way in exploring and colonizing what they called "the New World." The Indians fought back, but they were no match for Spanish guns or the strange diseases the Europeans brought with them. Within a few decades of Columbus's voyage, bold Spanish adventurers, or *conquistadors*, had conquered the islands of the Caribbean, as well as Mexico and Peru.

Perhaps the greatest conquistador was Hernán Cortés, conqueror of the Aztec Empire in Mexico. In the early 1530s, Cortés had heard reports of a gold-rich region north of Spain's Mexican territories. In 1533, he sailed north along Mexico's Pacific Coast, where he found a rocky, barren land. Cortés thought it was an island, but another expedition two years later proved that the land was a peninsula, separated by water from the Mexican mainland but stretching far to the north. The peninsula later became

known as *Baja* (lower) *California*. The land to the north was named *Alta* (upper) *California*. Today, Baja California remains part of Mexico. Alta California is the present-day state of California.

The first European explorer to set foot in Alta California was Juan Rodríguez de Cabrillo of Spain. Cabrillo's goal was to find the legendary Northwest Passage, a body of water thought to connect the Atlantic and Pacific oceans. In June 1542, Cabrillo's two-ship expedition sailed from the Mexican port of Navidad. Three months later the ships reached San Diego Bay. The explorers continued up the coast, landing at Catalina Island, San Pedro,

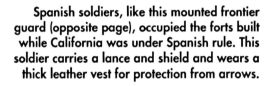
Spanish soldiers, like this mounted frontier guard (opposite page), occupied the forts built while California was under Spanish rule. This soldier carries a lance and shield and wears a thick leather vest for protection from arrows.

Native Americans greet Sir Francis Drake (above, right) as he lands in California. According to one of his officers, "the people of the country, having their houses close by the water's side, [showed] themselves unto us, and sent a present to our General [Drake]."

This map (right) shows the route taken by Father Eusebio Francisco Kino, a Jesuit priest who journeyed to California in 1701. Because Kino came to California overland by way of the Colorado and Gila rivers, he proved once and for all that the region was not an island.

Santa Monica, and San Miguel Island. When bad weather kept Cabrillo from sailing farther north, the expedition returned to San Miguel Island. There, in January 1543, Cabrillo died. Cabrillo's second-in-command, Bartolomé Ferrelo, renewed the voyage. The expedition sailed as far north as the region that is now Oregon, but illness and lack of food forced a return to Mexico.

The next Europeans to visit California came not from Spain, but from England. In 1579, the English sea captain Sir Francis Drake arrived off the California coast. His ship, the *Golden Hind*, was badly in need of repairs after many months at sea. Sailing through "stinking fogs" north of what is now San Francisco, Drake found "a convenient and fit harbor."

Drake spent about five weeks in California, enjoying the hospitality of the local Native Americans. Drake named the land *Nova Albion* ("New England" in Latin)—the cliffs around the bay reminded him of the white cliffs of Dover, England—and claimed it for Queen Elizabeth I.

England never followed up Drake's claim to California. For many years the Spanish also seemed to lose interest in the region. Not until 1602 did a major Spanish expedition arrive in California.

In that year, the Spanish government commanded Sebastián Vizcaíno to explore and map the entire California coast. Every year, a Spanish galleon (a large ship), crammed with riches from Spain's colonies in Asia, sailed across the Pacific to Mexico. It

was a long, hard voyage. Spanish officials hoped Vizcaíno would find a harbor where these ships could stop before making the final leg of the voyage to Mexico.

Sailing from Acapulco with three ships, Vizcaíno entered a large bay on December 16, 1602. He named it Monterey Bay after a Spanish nobleman. Vizcaíno didn't actually discover the bay—earlier explorers, including Cabrillo, had seen it. He was the first, however, to map the bay and the surrounding land.

Despite Vizcaíno's suggestions, Spain decided against founding settlements in California. For the next century and a half, California was left to the Native Americans.

Europeans were often curious about the customs of Native Americans and tried to document them. This engraving (opposite), from a book published in 1812, shows California Indians performing a ritual dance for a group of explorers. The dancers decorated themselves with paint, furs, feathers, and shells.

Russia established only one major outpost in California—Fort Ross, at Bodega Bay near San Francisco. This print (above) shows how the settlement looked in 1828. The small Russian fort was used as a base for fur-trading expeditions and lasted until 1841, when it was abandoned and sold.

The Missions

In 1765, José de Gálvez was made inspector-general of Spain's North American colonies. Gálvez used his authority to establish Spanish outposts in the region. In addition to expanding Spain's empire, he wanted to see California's Indians converted to the Catholic Church.

The job of colonizing California was given to Gaspar de Portolá, a soldier, and Father Junípero Serra, a priest of the Franciscan religious order. By summer of 1769, they had established a base camp at San Diego.

While Serra began building a mission—a religious settlement—in San Diego, de Portolá led fifty soldiers on a journey to explore the coast. Blazing a trail that became known as *El Camino Real* (the Royal Road), Portolá and his men journeyed as far as San Francisco Bay before returning to San Diego.

Before his death in 1784, the tireless Junípero Serra founded nine California missions along El Camino Real, each a day's journey from the last. The work continued after his death, until twenty-one missions had been built. These missions had a great influence on California history, and on the lives of California's Native Americans.

The missions were run by members of the Franciscan order. Each included a church, a school, storerooms, workshops, and houses, all built around a central courtyard, or patio. Outside were gardens, orchards, and pastures where cattle, brought from Mexico, could graze.

The Franciscan priests asked local Native Americans to leave their villages and move inside the missions. Many did. By the end of the 18th century, the California missions were home to more than 20,000 Native Americans.

But once they entered the mission gate, Native Americans had to give up their ancient way of life. The rituals of the Catholic Church replaced their traditional religious customs. And they no longer hunted or fished. Instead, the Franciscans taught the Indians to grow fruits and vegetables, to raise animals, and to take up European crafts such as carpentry and winemaking.

Mission life spelled an end to the freedom of Native Americans. Those who escaped from the missions were hunted down and forced to return. Discipline was often harsh, and whipping was a common punishment for misbehavior. A French explorer who visited the missions in the 1780s wrote that they made the Native American "too much a child, too much a slave, too little a man."

Health conditions in the missions were poor. European diseases such as

Founded in 1770, the mission of San Carlos de Borromeo de Monterey was the second mission established in California. In 1771, the mission was moved to nearby Carmel. In this drawing (above), Native Americans and priests welcome French explorer Jean François de Galaup La Pérouse to the mission in 1786.

Father Junípero Serra devoted much of his life to missionary activities among California's Native Americans. In this portrait (right) from a 1787 biography, Serra is shown in the simple garb of the Franciscan order.

smallpox and tuberculosis were brought to California by missionaries and soldiers. Because Native Americans had no natural defenses against these unfamiliar illnesses, they died in large numbers. These diseases also spread outside the missions, reducing the population of the Native Americans who still lived in California's mountains and valleys.

At the same time the missions were established, Spain was planting two other kinds of settlements throughout California—*presidios* and *pueblos.* Presidios were military posts manned by soldiers and their families. Pueblos were farming communities, settled mostly by *mestizos*—people of mixed Spanish and Native American blood— from Mexico. In the late 18th century a number of important presidios and pueblos were founded. They would later become the cities we know as San Francisco, San Jose, and Los Angeles. By 1781 only about 600 settlers lived in Alta California.

Native Americans who lived in the missions learned European arts and crafts. This *retablo* **(above, left)—a religious painting on wood— was created in 1783.**

Inspector-General José de Gálvez published this notice (left) to announce the 1769 expedition of Gaspar de Portolá and Junípero Serra. Monterey, site of the mission and presidio established in 1770, became the capital of Alta California in 1775.

The Ranches

Spain's power and wealth declined during the 18th century. When Spanish colonies in the New World began demanding independence early in the 19th century, Spain could do little to resist. In 1821, Mexico became independent. Now California would be ruled as a territory of Mexico.

The government in Mexico City was too far away to govern the *Californios*, as the settlers called themselves, and the 100,000 or so surviving Native Americans. The heads of the most powerful Californio families were the real rulers in California. They spent much of their time fighting each other in many "rebellions" and "revolutions," almost all of them bloodless.

The Mexican government did bring about one major change—the downfall of the missions. The Mexican authorities resented the power of the Franciscans who ran the missions. In 1833, a new Mexican law took control of the missions away from the Franciscans. Within a few years the missions fell into ruin. Some of the Native Americans who had lived in

This engraving shows a few of the 50,000 head of cattle owned by Mariano Vallejo, one of the wealthiest and most powerful Californio ranchers.

the missions tried to return to their old way of life. Others returned home, where conditions for them were even worse than in the missions. Some wound up working on the many new *ranchos*, or cattle ranches.

Vast herds of cattle grazed on the ranches, which could be as large as 50,000 acres. Twice a year, the cattle were rounded up and driven to the coast to be slaughtered. They were not able to sell much of the meat, because they had no refrigeration, but the rest of the cow was well used. The cowhides were dried in the sun. The fat was boiled into tallow. The tallow was shipped to South America to be made into candles and soap. The hides were sent around South Amer-

ica to New England, where they were turned into shoes and clothes. In return, the ranch owners received tools, money, furniture, and other goods.

Later writers and artists painted a romantic picture of ranch life. The hospitality of the ranch families was legendary. A guest was often treated to a week-long party, complete with elegant dances like the *fandango*. The horsemanship of the Californios was also famous. Today, Americans like to joke that Californians rarely leave their cars; visitors to ranches in the 1830s and 1840s, however, claimed that Californios spent their entire lives in the saddle.

But ranch life was leisurely and pleasant only for the owner and his family. The hard work was done by hundreds of Native American workers, who usually received only food and shelter in return. The ranch system also kept California backward in many ways. With no schools, few people could read and write. There were no large towns and practically no industry. Even simple items such as brooms had to be imported.

Meanwhile, more and more foreigners were arriving in California, attracted by offers of land. In order to receive a ranch grant, a newcomer needed only to accept Mexican citizenship and agree to become a Catholic. Many did, including Johann Augustus Sutter, who arrived in 1839 —the first to settle in the central valley. A former officer in the Swiss army, Sutter dreamed of building a private empire in northern California. Besides his ranch grant, Sutter bought the Russian-American Fur Company's land at Bodega Bay in 1841. This huge estate was called Sutter's Fort and it was a place of refuge for many foreigners arriving in California.

Most of the new Californians were Americans. Some settled in the coastal towns, acting as agents for the companies that bought the ranches' hides and tallow. Others established ranches themselves. Fur-trapping mountain men came into California over the Sierra Nevada. In 1841, the wagon train arrived, bringing American settlers to farm California's fertile valleys.

For members of the *gente de razón*, the 800 or so members of the richest rancho families, there was plenty of time for sports and parties. In this painting (opposite), Californios dance the spirited fandango.

This engraving (below) shows a typical Californio ranch worker. He wears equipment and clothing still used on ranches today, including a lariat for roping cattle and chaps to protect his legs while on horseback.

The Californios worried about the growing American interest in California. In the 1840s, Americans were talking eagerly about "Manifest Destiny," the belief that the United States had the right to spread across North America from the Atlantic to the Pacific. American settlers in the Mexican province of Texas had already won independence from Mexico in 1836, and Texas would soon be part of the United States. Why couldn't the same thing happen to California?

A strange incident in 1842 made Mexican Californians even more concerned. A U.S. Navy officer, Captain Thomas Catesby Jones, was at sea off the coast of Peru when he heard a

The early Californians were often wild and reckless. Their love of danger is illustrated in this print (above) which shows three Californios about to rope a cornered grizzly bear—a favorite sport.

rumor that Mexico and the United States were at war. Taking matters into his own hands he sailed to Monterey with a squadron of warships. When he came into the harbor, he ordered that the American flag be raised over the port. Out-gunned, the port authorities had to obey. One day after the "capture" of Monterey, official word from Mexico arrived. There was no war. Catesby apologized and sailed away. Soon, however, Americans and Californios would be at war.

The Bear Flag Republic

In 1844, James K. Polk was elected president of the United States. Polk was a strong believer in Manifest Destiny, and he soon set out to make California part of the United States. He offered to buy California and New Mexico from the Mexican government for $40 million, but the offer was rejected. Polk also encouraged the American settlers and native Californios to strive for independence from Mexico. An independent California, Polk hoped, would ask to join the United States.

Polk did get California, but not in the way he had planned. In the spring of 1846, a young U.S. Army officer named John C. Frémont arrived at Monterey. Frémont, already famous as an explorer, told the authorities that he was mapping a new route to California. The Californios, however, suspected that Frémont was there to make trouble. They were right.

By the 1840s the first American trappers, traders, and explorers had made their way west into Mexican California. This engraving (below) shows members of an American exploring expedition camped along the Sacramento River. Many Americans wanted the region to become part of the United States.

Frémont's father-in-law was Thomas Hart Benton, a powerful U.S. senator. Most historians believe that Benton wanted Frémont to lead a revolt against Mexican rule. Colonel José Castro ordered Frémont to leave California. But Frémont simply retreated into the mountains to wait for his chance.

That chance came a few months later. A small group of American settlers in the Napa and Sacramento valleys decided that the time was right for revolt. The Americans seized the town of Sonoma and proclaimed the founding of the California Republic. This short-lived nation soon became known as the Bear Flag Republic after one of the Americans, William B. Ide, designed a flag featuring a grizzly bear. When news of the revolt reached Frémont, he hurried south to take command.

Meanwhile, the United States and Mexico had gone to war. The two nations disagreed on the exact borders of Texas, and President Polk decided that war was the only way to seize California and other Mexican territories. In May 1846, at Polk's urging, Congress declared war on Mexico.

News traveled slowly in those days. Neither the Californios nor the "Bear Flaggers" knew about the war until July 2, when American warships commanded by Commodore John D. Sloat dropped anchor off Monterey. Marines went ashore to raise the American flag over the old presidio. By the end of the summer, all of Alta California was under United States control.

There was little resistance from the Californios, until the American officer in charge of Los Angeles placed the town under harsh military rule. Angry at this unfair treatment, a group of Californio officers rose up and drove the American troops out of Los Angeles. To the Americans' surprise, the Californios proved to be tough opponents. Soon much of southern California was in Californio hands.

In December, more American troops arrived—about 100 men commanded by General Stephen Watts Kearny. After a bitter fight near San Diego, Kearny marched on to recapture Los Angeles. Thirteen months later, a peace treaty ended the war between the United States and Mexico. Now it was official: California was American soil.

Thanks to the U.S. Navy, American forces were able to occupy California's coastal towns quickly. A U.S. warship lies at anchor off the California coast in this 1847 drawing by William Myers (opposite, top).

John C. Frémont plants the American flag on a mountain peak in this engraving (right). Frémont's reckless actions in California made him, in the words of historian H. H. Bancroft, "a popular hero, a senator of the United States, a millionaire . . . a major-general; [but] he was essentially a lucky fellow."

The Gold Rush

On January 24, 1848, a carpenter named James Marshall was building a sawmill on Johann Sutter's land in the foothills of the Sierra Nevada. Out of the corner of his eye, Marshall saw something glitter beneath the surface of the American River. It was a small yellow rock. Could it be gold? Marshall rode to Sutter's Fort, where Sutter tested the rock. It was indeed gold—high-quality gold. Fearing a stampede of treasure-hunters on his land, Sutter tried to keep Marshall's discovery a secret. But word of the find soon leaked out. "Gold fever" swept the coastal towns.

Soon people from all over the world were heading to California to try their luck in the mining camps. The great California Gold Rush was on. About 12,000 people lived in California in 1848, not including the Native Americans. By 1852, thanks to the Gold Rush, there would be more than 250,000. Because the greatest number of immigrants arrived in 1849, the gold-seekers would forever be known as "forty-niners."

The forty-niners were mostly young men. Few planned to stay in California—most hoped to strike it rich and head home. Many were Americans, but large groups also came from China, Australia, Europe, and South America. There weren't many women among the forty-niners, since condi-

This 1850 lithograph shows Sutter's Mill, center, on the south fork of the American River—site of the discovery that sparked the great Gold Rush. At left, the mining town of Coloma spans both banks of the river.

tions were rough and mining gold was not thought to be a job for a woman.

There were three ways to get to California from the eastern United States. The first was by ship, all the way around the tip of South America and up to San Francisco. Depending on the ship's speed, the trip could take anywhere from ten weeks to eight months. A second route was by ship via the Isthmus of Panama, the narrow strip of land between the Atlantic and Pacific. Travelers would then board a northbound ship on the other side.

Most immigrants came to California by land. They traveled across the deserts and mountains of the West in vast convoys of wagons. The overland route was a long, hard journey, but it was usually cheaper than either of the sea routes. Once in California, the prospectors swarmed into mining camps with colorful names like Hell's Delight and Poker Flats.

The forty-niners soon discovered that gold mining was hard, back-

Life in the mining camps was usually primitive and harsh. In this drawing (right), miners sleep in bunkbeds in a crowded boarding house. Others lived in tents and dugouts.

Eager fortune hunters use airships and rockets to get to California in this 1849 cartoon (below). The first forty-niners reached San Francisco aboard the steamship California in February 1849. Although the ship was only supposed to carry 200 passengers, twice as many gold-seekers managed to cram aboard.

breaking work. The most common mining method, panning, meant squatting in a river or stream all day, swirling dirt and water together in a frying pan. The water washed the sand away, leaving the heavier flecks of gold in the bottom of the pan.

A few forty-niners did strike it rich—one twelve-year-old miner found $2,700 worth of gold in just two days. Most, however, found only disappointment. Some gave up and went home. Others turned to gambling and alcohol. But many stayed on to make a new life in California.

Many immigrants, in fact, made fortunes not from gold, but from serving the needs of the gold miners. Because food and other goods had to be brought to California over long distances, prices were high. A loaf of bread could cost $2—a huge price in those days. Anyone with goods to sell could make a great profit. Levi Strauss, for example, began his clothing empire by selling tough, comfortable denim pants to miners.

If the Gold Rush brought disappointment to most forty-niners, it brought tragedy to California's original citizens. Californios and Indians lost much of their land. Because California had no real government at this time, there was little these people could do to keep trespassing miners off their property. Johann Sutter watched helplessly as forty-niners ruined his land—just as he had feared.

STATEHOOD AND BEYOND

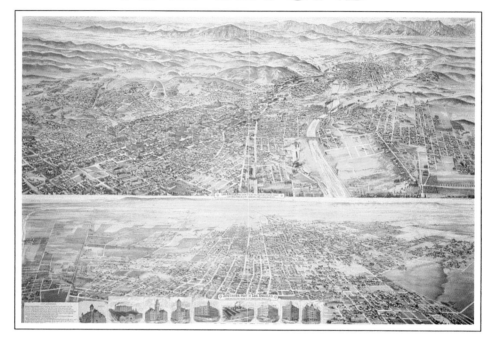

This print shows Los Angeles in 1894, two years after an oil strike inside the city limits led to a real estate boom.

In 1850, California became the thirty-first state of the Union. Over the next seven decades, both California's cities and rural areas developed at a fast pace. Farming, tourism, manufacturing, and the movie industry combined to make the state an economic powerhouse. Although hard-hit by the depression of the 1930s, the state prospered during World War II and began an era of spectacular growth in the 1950s. By 1962, California was the nation's most populous state. But rapid growth brought problems of pollution, overcrowding, and social unrest—problems the state is still grappling with in the 1990s.

Statehood

When the Mexican War ended, most Americans thought California would follow the usual path to statehood. This meant that Congress would first organize California as a territory. Then, when California's voting population reached 60,000, it could draw up a constitution and ask to be admitted to the Union as a new state. This process was expected to take years. The discovery of gold in 1848, however, changed everything.

Because of the Gold Rush, California's population reached the number required to apply for statehood in 1849. With so many people pouring into California, there was a desperate need for government. President Zachary Taylor recognized this need. At his urging, a constitutional convention was called, to be held in Monterey in September 1849. Elections were held throughout California to choose delegates.

When the convention met, it made three important decisions. First, the delegates decided to ask to join the

Isolated from the rest of the nation, Californians waited anxiously while politicians in Washington debated the territory's request for admission to the Union. When news of statehood reached San Francisco, joyful citizens celebrated with parades, speeches, and fireworks (below).

Union as a state, skipping the territory stage. Second, the convention voted to apply for statehood as a single state. Many delegates from part of the territory favored splitting California into two new states. Southern Californians feared that northern California would dominate the new state. However, the southern delegates didn't have enough votes to win approval for their proposal. Third, and probably most important, the delegates voted to forbid slavery in California.

The convention's decision sparked a national political crisis. At this time, there was much tension between the Southern states, which allowed slavery, and the Northern states, where slavery was outlawed. The results of

the Mexican War in 1847 made these tensions worse. Many Northerners feared that the lands won from Mexico would be opened to slavery when they became territories and then states. Southerners, on the other hand, feared that these new states would outlaw slavery.

For these reasons, many Southern politicians fought against California's request to be admitted to the Union. After a long, bitter debate, Congress settled on a compromise. California would be admitted as a free state. The issue of slavery in the rest of the lands won from Mexico would be decided later.

Peter H. Burnett became the state's first governor. San Jose was the original state capital, but the state government moved several times before settling in Sacramento in 1854.

The Gold Rush was mostly over by then, but California continued to grow in the 1850s. People from many nations poured into the new state. One large group of immigrants came from China. Chinese immigration had begun during the Gold Rush. By 1852, the Chinese made up 10 percent of the state's population. More and more of these settlers were families, increasing the number of women in the new state. By the end of the decade the state's population was almost 380,000.

The distance between California and the rest of the nation made communications difficult. To speed things up, the famous Pony Express began business in 1860. Using relays of young riders on fast horses, the service could carry a letter from St. Joseph, Missouri, to San Francisco in ten days. A telegraph line soon linked California with the East.

In April 1861, four months before the telegraph line reached California, the conflict over slavery boiled over into civil war between the Northern and Southern states. California remained in the Union, supporting the Northern side of the war. About 500 Californians went east to join the Union Army as the "California Battalion." California, however, was too far away from the fighting to play much of a part in the war.

The new state included people from all over the world. This 1855 engraving (above) depicts gold miners, Mexican-Californian *vaqueros* (cowboys), and Chinese laborers in a San Francisco saloon. Probably a quarter of California's population was foreign-born during the first decades of statehood.

A Pony Express rider greets workers stringing telegraph wire in this engraving (opposite page) from *Harper's Weekly*. The telegraph finally reached California in October 1861, ending the brief life of the Pony Express.

The Railroads

The telegraph didn't solve the problem of California's isolation. The telegraph carried only words. People and products going to or from California still faced a long, rough journey by ship or wagon train.

A young engineer named Theodore Judah believed that he had the answer. Judah proposed a transcontinental railroad—a rail line that would link the Pacific Coast with the rest of the nation. Some people scoffed at Judah's idea. Such a railroad would have to cross mountains thousands of feet high, burning deserts, and the endless plains of the West. But Judah, who had built California's first railroad in 1854–56, was sure this feat could be done.

In 1861, Judah founded the Central Pacific Railroad Company. He needed money, so he looked for business people to support his dream. He found four financial backers—Charles Crocker, Mark Hopkins, Collis P. Huntington, and Leland Stanford. All four men had come from the East and made fortunes as merchants during the Gold Rush.

Even with the financial help of the "Big Four," as his partners came to be called, Judah still didn't have enough money to begin work. Soon, however, the federal government realized that a transcontinental railroad would benefit the entire nation. On July 1, 1862,

President Abraham Lincoln signed the Pacific Railroad Act into law. The bill provided up to $48,000 of government money to the Central Pacific for every mile of track it built. In addition, the bill gave the company grants of government-owned land along the railroad's route.

On January 8, 1863, the Central Pacific Company began laying track east from Sacramento. The company's goal was to link up with the Union Pacific Railroad, which was working its way west from Nebraska. Not long after work began, however, Theodore Judah resigned from the company after an argument with his partners. On his way east, he fell sick and died in New York City.

Over the next six years, the Central Pacific moved slowly but steadily eastward. The difficulties were great, especially when the tracks crossed the Sierra Nevada. Tunnels and ledges had to be blasted through solid rock. The hard, dangerous work was done mostly by Chinese workers. The Central Pacific brought more than 20,000 laborers from China to keep the steel rails moving east.

Finally, on May 10, 1869, the tracks of the Central Pacific and the Union Pacific met at Promontory Point in the Utah Territory. California's isolation from the rest of the country was over at last.

"Across the Continent" is the title of this Currier & Ives lithograph (above) celebrating the transcontinental railroad. New towns sprouted up across the plains, dramatically changing the landscape.

In addition to building a railroad empire, New York-born Leland Stanford (right) served as California's governor (1862–63) and as a U.S. senator (1885–93). In 1885, he founded Stanford University, now one of the nation's leading educational institutions, to honor a son who had died.

Growing Pains

Most Californians believed the transcontinental railroad would bring new prosperity to their state. In fact, the railroad had the opposite effect. By making it much cheaper to bring goods into California, the railroad caused prices to fall. Many businesses went bankrupt. In addition, many banks failed because of unwise investments in depleted silver mines in Nevada. The 1870s were hard years for the people of California.

In the face of hardship, many Californians looked for someone to blame. They found the Chinese. Because Chinese immigrants were often forced to work for low wages, non-Chinese Californians feared competition for scarce jobs. Many towns organized anti-Chinese societies.

Prejudice against the Chinese soon turned into violence. Nineteen Chinese immigrants were killed by a mob in Los Angeles in 1871. Similar attacks took place in 1877 in San Francisco, home of an anti-Chinese political group called the Workingmen's Party. This and other groups demanded an end to Chinese immigration. In 1882, they got their wish: Congress passed a law forbidding Chinese people to come to the United States. The law remained in effect for many years.

Despite the prejudice and violence Chinese immigrants encountered when they first arrived in the 1840s, they continued to come to California in the 1870s. This engraving (left) shows Chinese immigrants arriving in San Francisco in 1877—five years before a federal law outlawed Chinese immigration altogether.

This newspaper illustration (opposite page) shows Modoc rebels shooting General Edward S. Canby on April 11, 1873. The six-month campaign against the Modocs cost the U.S. Army nearly $1 million and the lives of eighty-three soldiers.

The 1870s also saw the last stand of California's Native Americans. During the Gold Rush, the Native Americans lost what little land they had left. In the 1850s and 1860s, thousands of Native Americans died from disease or from attacks by white settlers. The survivors were forced to live on reservations. Historian H. H. Bancroft described this period as "One of the last human hunts of civilization, and . . . the most brutal of them all."

One group, the Modoc tribe, fought back. The Modocs originally lived in northern California, just below the Oregon border. In the 1850s, the U.S. Army forced the Modocs off their land and onto a reservation. In 1872, the surviving Modocs, about 175 people in all, escaped from the reservation and set off for their homeland. Their leader was Kientepoos, or "Captain Jack," as the whites called him. Four hundred soldiers chased the Modocs into the area around Tule Lake. The Modocs were able to hide in this rugged region, and they fought so fiercely that the army called a peace conference. Unfortunately, Modoc warriors killed an army general and a Methodist missionary at the meeting. The attack ruined any chance for a peaceful settlement. The soldiers stormed the Modoc hiding places and forced the survivors back to the reservation. Kientepoos was captured and hanged in 1873.

By the end of the 1870s, California again began to prosper. Farming was the key to the state's renewed growth. At first, wheat was California's most valuable crop. It was grown mostly on large farms in the Central Valley region between the state's major mountain ranges. In northern California, immigrants from Europe began growing grapes and producing wine. By 1900, four-fifths of all the wine made in the United States came from California, especially from vineyards in the Napa and Sonoma valleys.

It was southern California that grew the most in the years before the turn of the 19th century. Much of the land was owned by railroads, including the Southern Pacific, which was part of the Big Four's transportation empire. In the 1880s, the railroads offered land at low prices to immigrants from the East and overseas. Hundreds of thousands of people, including the first Japanese immigrants, traveled to California to buy land and start farms.

To make it easy for people to come to the state, the railroads cut their fares to record lows. At one point, a person could ride from Missouri to Los Angeles for $1. Books and posters advertised the delights of southern California. Soon the state was swept up in a land boom that seemed like a second Gold Rush. Land values around Los Angeles doubled overnight and then doubled again. In 1880, about 11,000 people lived in Los Angeles. By 1888, the year the land boom ended, the city's population stood at almost 80,000.

As Los Angeles grew, its citizens realized the city needed a deep-water port to complete its transportation network. Most businesspeople wanted to expand the harbor facilities at San Pedro. The Southern Pacific Company, led by Collis Huntington, favored Santa Monica as the site for the new port. The controversy over where to build lasted until 1899 when Santa Monica was chosen. The port, one of the largest artificial harbors ever built, was completed in 1910.

Many of the newcomers planted oranges and other citrus fruits, which grew well in California's sunny climate. In 1886, the first trainload of California oranges rolled east to market. Within a few years, the state was producing two-thirds of the nation's oranges and almost all of its lemons.

Because of low rainfall in much of the state, California farmers had to depend on irrigation. This meant that water had to be brought to wheat fields and citrus groves from lakes and rivers, often over great distances. Thanks to irrigation, California became a major producer of vegetables, cotton, and other crops. But irrigation also brought problems. Moving water through canals and pipelines often damaged the environment. Irrigation also led to conflict over the control of water rights. These problems continue today.

California's growth in the last decades of the 19th century brought new opportunities for women. In this photograph (above), an ox-team driver known as "Arizona Mary" is shown at work in southern California.

This poster (right) was one of many published to attract immigrants to California during the land boom of the late 1880s. At the height of the boom, the price of an acre of farmland in one county of southern California jumped from $350 to $10,000 in a single year.

The Twentieth Century

California's population reached 1.5 million as the 20th century dawned. San Francisco remained the state's largest and most important city. With a population of about 500,000, San Francisco was the sixth-largest city in the United States.

In 1906, disaster struck San Francisco. Earthquakes have always been a problem in California, because the state is crossed by many fault lines—areas where huge sheets of underground rock meet. At daybreak on April 18, one of these fault lines shifted beneath San Francisco, and for about ninety seconds the city shook wildly. Houses were ripped from their foundations. Buildings toppled into the streets.

The earthquake was just the beginning of the disaster. Soon, fires broke out. The quake had shattered water pipes, so the city's firefighters could do little to stop the flames from spreading. The blaze took three days to die down. Together, the San Francisco earthquake and fire claimed 700 lives. Almost 30,000 buildings—two-thirds of the entire city—lay in ruins.

The fires were barely out before the city began to rebuild. The pace of the reconstruction was rapid: Within a

decade of the disaster, San Francisco was back on its feet.

While San Francisco rebuilt, southern California and Los Angeles continued to grow. The discovery of oil in Los Angeles County led to yet another boom. Also, thousands of tourists came to the area, attracted by its scenery and climate, and many decided to stay.

As always, growth brought problems to California. Labor troubles hit California in the first decades of the 20th century. Industry was now an important part of the state's economy. In those days, however, few laws protected workers. Many people—including women and small children—had to work long hours in dangerous factories for low wages. Workers banded together into labor unions, using

Dazed citizens watch in horror as fire sweeps through San Francisco after the great earthquake of 1906 (opposite page). Together, the earthquake and fire leveled almost 500 acres of the city.

By 1900, industrial mining of petroleum, iron ore, and cement minerals had replaced much of the mining of precious metals like gold and silver. This picture (above, right) shows drilling towers in an oil field in southern California.

California's natural treasures attracted growing numbers of tourists in the early years of the 20th century. The state's landscape offered a variety of pleasures—sun and sand to the south and mountains and woodlands to the north. In this photograph (right), a wagonload of visitors passes through one of the famous giant redwoods of Mariposa Grove.

strikes and other tactics to seek better working conditions. Sometimes the conflict between labor and business boiled over into violence.

In 1910, Hiram Johnson, a lawyer sympathetic to the labor movement, was elected governor. He eased the state's labor conflicts by passing laws establishing basic rights for workers.

A new form of entertainment—the movies—also made its mark on California. In 1907, movie production companies started moving from the East Coast to southern California. The area offered many advantages to the new industry. Outdoor filming could go on all year long in the region's sunny weather. Movie makers could find any kind of scenery they needed, from mountains to deserts, within a few hour's drive from Los Angeles. In 1913, director Cecil B. deMille filmed a movie in the small town of Hollywood. Soon, Hollywood was the capital of the nation's movie industry.

THE ABDUCTION.

THE ECLECTIC FILM COMPANY'S GREAT $25,000 PRIZE PHOTO PLAY

THE PERILS OF PAULINE

6TH EPISODE IN 2 PARTS

Under the leadership of Hiram Johnson (above, left), the progressive movement in California passed twenty-two reform amendments to the state constitution. In 1912, Johnson ran unsuccessfully for the vice presidency of the United States on the Progressive Party's ticket.

Early movies tended to be short comedies or melodramas, like the one advertised in this poster (left). By the end of the 1920s, the motion-picture industry was the tenth-largest industry in the United States and an important part of California's economy.

The Twenties and the Depression

By 1920, almost 3.5 million people lived in California. In that year, Los Angeles bypassed San Francisco to become the largest city in the state. By the decade's end, the population had grown by 2.25 million.

San Diego took its place as one of California's major cities during this time. Although San Diego was the site of the first Spanish settlement in California, it had always lagged behind San Francisco and Los Angeles in development and population. This began to change in 1915, when the Panama Canal opened for business. The canal gave ships a shortcut between the Atlantic and Pacific oceans across the Isthmus of Panama. Thanks to the canal, San Diego became an important port and the site of a major base for the U.S. Navy. The city was also home to much of the state's new aircraft industry. In 1922, Kansas-born Claude Ryan started the Ryan Flying Company in San Diego. Soon, the company began flying people between Los Angeles and San Diego —the first regular air passenger service in the country. The Ryan Company also built the *Spirit of St. Louis*, the plane Charles Lindbergh piloted in his famous flight from New York to Paris in 1927.

The United States prospered in the 1920s, and so did California. But in 1929, a stock market collapse, which led to the sudden failure of many businesses and banks, plunged the nation into a long period of hard economic times known as the Great Depression. The Depression struck California hard. Businesses closed throughout the state. Many small farmers lost their land. By 1934, one in five Californians was out of work.

In that year, writer Upton Sinclair won the Democratic Party's nomination for governor. Sinclair hoped to bring California out of the Depression through a plan called EPIC (End Poverty in California). Among other things, EPIC called for the state government to take over farms and factories that had gone out of business, providing jobs for the unemployed and food for the hungry. Sinclair's opponents, Republican Frank Merriam and Progressive Raymond Haight, called EPIC a dangerous, radical program. Merriam and Haight used the support of California's powerful movie industry during the campaign to run short films attacking Sinclair and EPIC. Merriam won the three-way election, but many of the ideas Upton Sinclair put forward in EPIC were later adopted by California's government.

Another Californian with a plan to end the miseries of the Depression

was Francis Townsend, a doctor from Long Beach. Townsend's idea, which he announced in 1933, involved giving a monthly pension of $200 to all residents over sixty. The state government would pay for the pensions by taxing businesses; every person receiving money would have to spend it in a month.

Townsend believed his scheme would make life better for the state's senior citizens while boosting the state's economy. Townsend wasn't able to win enough political support to put his idea into action. Although a similar plan gained popularity a few years later, it was defeated in a special election and was never adopted by the state government.

As the Depression worsened, labor unrest spread through California's industrial areas. Longshoremen —workers who load cargo on and off ships—suffered especially. They endured low pay and dangerous working conditions. In 1934, labor leader Harry Bridges led a strike of dockworkers in San Francisco, shutting the port down. When warehouse and ship owners hired strikebreakers to move cargo, the strike turned violent. On July 5, "Bloody Thursday," two longshoremen were killed and over 250 people were wounded in clashes between strikers and strikebreakers.

As bad as things were in California, they were worse elsewhere. Years of drought in the western states caused

conditions in which soil dried up and blew away. Between 1935 and 1939, at least 350,000 people left these "dust bowl" states for California. Because many of these people came from Oklahoma, these newcomers were known as Okies.

Many found work as laborers on the huge corporate farms of the San Joaquin Valley. There, Okies had to live in crowded, unhealthy camps. Entire families did backbreaking work for pay that barely bought enough food to eat. *The Grapes of Wrath*, a powerful novel by John Steinbeck, drew national attention to the plight of the Okies. The farm owners, however, fought every attempt to improve conditions for the migrant workers.

California took an early lead in the aviation industry. In 1911, pilot Glenn Curtiss made the first successful seaplane flight near San Diego; a year later, one of the first airmail services began running between Compton and Santa Ana. This photograph (opposite page) shows passengers boarding a Curtiss Condor airliner in the 1920s.

In 1936, Dorothea Lange took this haunting photograph (above) of migrant workers arriving in California. The work of Lange and other Farm Security Administration photographers helped convince California's government to build camps that would house and feed some of the thousands of migrants who were pouring into the state.

World War II and After

World War II finally pulled California out of the Depression. The war had already raged for years in Europe and Asia when Japan attacked the U.S. Navy base at Pearl Harbor in Hawaii on December 7, 1941.

Almost overnight, California industry went into high gear to provide ships, planes, food, and other products for the American war effort. Factories and shipyards that had closed during the Depression opened again, and many more were built. From all over the United States, people moved to California to work in its wartime industries. For the first time in California's history, large numbers of African Americans arrived in the state hoping to find jobs. To meet the increased demand for food, the American and Mexican governments developed the *Bracero* program. Taking its name from a Spanish term meaning "strong-armed ones," the program brought thousands of Mexicans to California to work on the state's farms.

Because California was the part of the United States closest to the fighting in the Pacific, many Californians feared that the state would be the target of a Japanese attack. False reports of air raids caused panic in Los Angeles in the early days of the conflict.

A Japanese submarine did fire some shells into an oil field near Santa Barbara, but this was the only such attack during the war.

For the 93,000 Japanese Americans in California, the war years were a terrible time. In the nervous months following Pearl Harbor, many people feared that Japanese Americans would try to damage the U.S. war effort.

In February 1942, an executive order from President Franklin Roosevelt cleared the way for the "evacuation" of Japanese Americans from the coastal areas of California, Oregon, and Washington. The army moved these people to what were called relocation centers at Tule Lake, Manzanar, and other inland sites. In these grim camps, Japanese Americans lived in crowded wooden barracks behind barbed wire. Finally, in late 1944, the government allowed the Japanese Americans to return to their home. Many, however, had no homes to return to. Most had had no choice but to sell their houses, businesses, and farms when the "evacuation" began.

The removal of the Japanese Americans was one of the worst violations of civil rights in American history. After the war, the government realized it had made a mistake. Congress

This portrait (above) shows a Japanese-American family waiting to be moved to a relocation camp in 1942. In addition to taking away their freedom, the relocation program cost California's Japanese Americans as much as half a billion dollars in property losses. Even as their families were imprisoned in the internment camps, many Japanese Americans volunteered and fought bravely in World War II.

The number of industrial workers in California jumped from 380,000 to more than 1 million during the years of World War II. Many of the new factory workers were women taking the place of men in the armed forces, as shown by this poster (right). W.O.W. stands for "Woman Ordnance Worker."

"THE GIRL HE LEFT BEHIND" IS STILL BEHIND HIM
She's a WOW
WOMAN ORDNANCE WORKER

later passed laws paying Japanese Americans for their lost property, but few regained all they had lost.

World War II ended in August 1945, and a new and amazing chapter in California's history began. Between 1950 and 1960, the state's population went from about 10.5 million to almost 16 million. California's cities grew at an unbelievable pace, and rings of suburbs grew up around the cities. A network of highways spread through the state, connecting cities to cities, and cities to suburbs.

What brought all these people to California? Jobs, for one thing. The state's industries flourished in the 1950s and early 1960s. New "high tech" businesses started up to serve the new space program and the military. These businesses brought large numbers of engineers, technicians, and other skilled workers to the state.

But there was something else that made people want to come to California. "It's not the better job that I'm interested in alone," said one new arrival in the 1950s, "It's the way of life." Some called it the California Dream—a chance to own a home and to work and play in the sunshine.

Cattle graze in the shadow of oil wells in Orange County in this 1942 photograph (below). Oil production in California increased by 50 percent during World War II.

The Problems of Growth

But the California Dream was an impossible dream for many of the state's people. Large parts of the population did not share in the prosperity of the postwar years.

Among these groups were the laborers who worked on California's farms. Most of the state's farms were huge parcels of land owned and run by big corporations. These farms needed the labor of many people to grow and harvest crops of fruit, vegetables, and grapes. By the 1960s, most farm workers were Mexicans or Americans of Mexican ancestry. They faced many problems—hard work, low pay, and poor living conditions.

In 1962, a young Mexican American, Cesar Chavez, founded the National Farm Workers Association (NFWA). By joining many workers

Cesar Chavez (above, right) led farmworkers in a strike in 1965. A follower described him as "poor like us, dark like us, moving people to talk about their problems. We didn't know until we met him, but he was the leader we had been waiting for."

Buttons like this one (right) urged Americans to boycott (refuse to buy) products like lettuce and grapes until growers agreed to recognize the rights of agricultural workers. Chavez forced the farm owners to meet the National Farm Workers demands by gaining the sympathy and support of millions of Americans.

together, Chavez and other farm-union organizers fought to win better treatment for farm laborers.

For California's African Americans, the 1960s were years of unrest. Between 1950 and 1960, more African Americans moved to California than to any other state. While most newcomers to California lived in small cities or suburbs, African Americans often found themselves unwelcome in these mostly white communities. Thus, most of the state's African Americans wound up living in crowded ghettos within big cities, like the Watts neighborhood in Los Angeles.

In August 1965, Watts exploded into rioting after white police officers arrested a young African American for drunk driving. The violence lasted for three days and claimed thirty-four lives. The riot forced the state to take a hard look at the problems of its African-American citizens, but there were no easy answers to California's racial problems.

Unrest also swept California's colleges and universities. Student protests against the Vietnam War took place on many campuses. Many people felt the state was spinning out of control. In 1966, citizens elected former movie actor Ronald Reagan governor. A conservative Republican, Reagan pledged to end the unrest on the state's college campuses.

The huge migration of people to California put the state government in a difficult position. The state had to spend millions of dollars to maintain

schools, roads, and other services for so many newcomers, plus providing welfare and medical care for California's poorer citizens. But raising money meant raising taxes, something that Reagan didn't want to do. By 1971, however, the state was so short of money that Reagan had to sign a large tax increase into law. The money problems continued after Edmund "Jerry" Brown, a liberal Democrat, was elected governor.

Money was only one of the problems facing California as the 1970s ended. Pollution was on the rise, thanks to the millions of cars and thousands of factories in the state. California's natural resources, especially its water supply, were under strain because of population growth. The very things that had brought so many to California—clean air and beautiful scenery—seemed in danger.

Northern California's "Silicon Valley" became home to many high-tech businesses in the 1970s and 1980s. In this photograph (above), Cupertino-based Apple Computer founders Stephen Wozniak, left, and Stephen Jobs, right, pose with a circuit board of one of the company's first computers.

During the 1960s and 1970s, student demonstrations against the Vietnam War were a common sight at California's colleges. The first major protests against the war, like the one shown here (opposite page), took place at the University of California at Berkeley in 1964.

California, Present and Future

The California state government addressed the issues of pollution by passing a series of environmental laws designed to preserve the coastline, add state park lands, and improve air quality. By the 1980s, California had adopted the strictest smog regulations in the United States.

In the early part of the decade, California's economy improved, although unemployment remained high in many communities. The state's population continued to grow, with an average of 500,000 new Californians arriving each year in the 1980s. Many came from Vietnam, Korea, China, and other Asian countries. Others came from Latin America, especially Mexico.

Natural disasters continued to hit California. Within a five-year period, two major earthquakes jolted the state. In 1989 the San Francisco Bay area was rocked by its largest earthquake since 1906. Sixty-seven people were killed, and there was $10 billion in damage. An earthquake of similiar magnitude hit Los Angeles in January 1994, bringing with it a death toll of sixty-one and property damage of close to $30 billion.

Besides the constant threat of earthquakes, California is plagued by annual brushfires. The fires begin when the Santa Ana winds—hot winds moving west from the desert—dry out the natural vegetation. Even a small spark can quickly become a raging fire.

Los Angeles was a city in the midst of great change as the 1990s began. The gap between rich and poor citizens grew, especially after a nationwide recession set in during the 1990s. People from different ethnic groups struggled to get along with each other. A high crime rate, overcrowded schools, and other problems plagued the city.

Los Angeles's African-American community had never recovered from the damages caused by the 1965 Watts riot. Many of the businesses that were destroyed had not been rebuilt or replaced. Poor neighborhoods offered few services and even fewer jobs. In addition, many African Americans felt the city's mostly white police force treated them unfairly.

Tensions worsened in March 1991, when a passerby videotaped four white policemen beating Rodney King, an African-American motorist, who had led them on a high-speed chase. The tape, which was shown on national television, stunned the country, and the four officers were put on trial for assault. On April 29, 1992, a suburban jury found the four police-men not guilty.

The verdict shocked most Americans and enraged Los Angeles's poor minority communities. Rioting broke out, and the violence spread throughout the city as more and more people joined in the looting and destruction. When the smoke cleared, three days later, fifty-three people were dead and 2,400 others injured. Property damage totaled more than $1 billion.

Many people wondered if the California Dream was over. Besides racial tensions, the state faced environmental problems and a sluggish economy—thousands of middle class Californians lost their jobs. Perhaps the state was no longer a place where people from all over America could find a better life. Californians of all kinds insist the dream is still alive and are seeking new solutions to the problems of the state and its cities.

Because of its size and importance, California has long been an example for the rest of the United States. In the words of poet Richard Armour, "What California is today, The rest will be tomorrow."

Thus, the entire nation is watching closely as California strives to build a better future for its citizens.

Sand, surf, and sun—the popular image of California—still attract visitors and new residents to the state. In this photograph, surfers take to the water at Orange County's Laguna Beach (below).

Land area:
158,706 square miles, of which 2,407 are inland water. Ranks 3rd in size.

Major rivers:
The Sacramento and San Joaquin river systems; the American; the Colorado; the Feather; the Kern; the Klamath; the Owens; the Russian.

Highest point: Mount Whitney, 14,494 ft. (highest point in the lower 48 states).

Climate:
Average January temperature: 57°F
Average July temperature: 74°F

Major bodies of water:
Goose Lake; Honey Lake; the Salton Sea; Lake Tahoe; Clair Engle Lake; Lake Mathews; Shasta Lake.

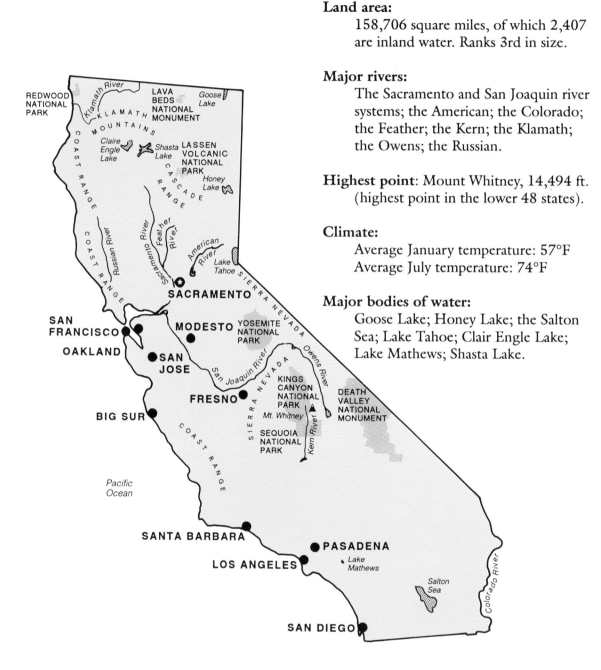

Population: 30,866,851 (1992)
Rank: 1st
    1850: 92,597
    1900: 1,485,053

Population of major cities (1992):

Los Angeles	3,485,398
San Diego	1,110,554
San Jose	782,248
San Francisco	723,959
Oakland	372,242

Ethnic breakdown by percentage (1990):

White	57.2%
Hispanic	25.8%
African American	7.0%
Asian	9.1%
Native American	0.6%
Other	0.3%

Economy:
Agriculture (cotton, beef and dairy products, lettuce, grapes, citrus fruits), wine making, timber products, fish, natural gas, manufacturing (aircraft, electronics, processed foods and beverages, clothing), entertainment, and tourism.

State government:
Legislature: Assembly has 80 members and senate has 40 members. Senators serve 4-year terms; assembly representatives serve 2-year terms.
Governor: Heading the executive branch, the governor is elected for a 4-year term.
Courts: California has a 3-level court system, including supreme, appellate, and trial courts.
State capital: Sacramento

State Flag

Adopted in 1911, California's state flag closely resembles the famous "Bear Flag" of the California Republic, designed by American settler William Todd in 1846.

State Seal

The figures representing California are Minerva, the Ancient Roman goddess of wisdom; a gold miner; and the Sierra Nevada. Thirty-one stars form an arch over the state motto at the top.

State Motto

"Eureka," which is Greek for "I've found it." This refers to the finding of gold in 1848, perhaps the most important discovery in California's history.

State Nickname

"The Golden State." The nickname was partly inspired by the Gold Rush.

Places

Alcatraz State Park, San Francisco Bay

Asian Art Museum, San Francisco

Big Sur, Monterey

California Academy of Science, San Francisco

California Museum of Science and Industry, Los Angeles

Cabrillo National Monument, Point Loma

Channel Islands National Monument, Los Angeles

Chinatown, San Francisco

Crocker Art Museum, Sacramento

Death Valley National Monument, near Darwin

Devil's Postpile National Monument, June Lake

Disneyland, Anaheim

El Pueblo de Los Angeles, Los Angeles

Fishermen's Wharf, San Francisco

Golden Gate Bridge, San Francisco

Hollywood, Los Angeles

Huntington Library and Botanical Gardens, San Marino

J. Paul Getty Museum, Malibu

Joshua Tree National Monument, Twentynine Palms

Kings Canyon National Park, East of Fresno

Knott's Berry Farm, Buena Park

to See

Hearst Castle
San Simeon,
near San Luis Obispo

La Brea Tar Pits,
Los Angeles

Lake Tahoe,
Tahoe City

**Lassen Volcanic
National Park,**
Mineral

**Lava Beds National
Monument,**
near Tule Lake

**Los Angeles County
Museum of Art,**
Los Angeles

**Marineland
of the Pacific,**
Hermosa Beach

**Mission Basilica San
Carlos Borremeo,**
Carmel

**Mission San Juan
Capistrano,**
San Capistrano

**Mission San Luis
Rey de Francia,**
Oceanside

**Muir Woods
National
Monument,**
Mill Valley

**Natural History
Museum of San
Diego,** San Diego

**Palomar
Observatory,**
San Diego

**Pinnacles National
Monument,** Soledad

**Redwood National
Park,** Crescent City

**San Diego Zoo,
Balboa Park,**
San Diego

**Santa Barbara
Museum of National
History,**
Santa Barbara

**State Capitol
Building,**
Sacramento

**Sequoia National
Park,** Three Rivers

**Yosemite
National Park**

State Flower

California's legislature named the golden poppy the official state flower in 1903. California's Native Americans used parts of the flower for food and cosmetics.

State Bird

The California valley quail became the state's official bird in 1931.

State Tree

The coast redwood and the giant sequoia were declared the official state trees of California in 1937. Coast redwoods are among the tallest trees on earth and they grow only in a narrow belt of land north of San Francisco.

California History

1542 Juan Cabrillo reaches San Diego Bay

1579 Francis Drake lands near San Francisco

1602 Sebastían Vizcaíno charts California's coast

1769 Mission founded at San Diego

1776 Colony established at San Francisco

1781 Los Angeles is founded

1821 Mexico achieves independence from Spain; California accepts Mexican rule in 1822

1841 First American settlers arrive overland in California

1846–47 American settlers proclaim independence; U.S. forces take control of California during the Mexican War

1848 Mexico transfers California territory to U.S.
• Gold found at Sutter's Mill

1849 The Gold Rush swells the region's population

1850 California is admitted to the Union

1854 Sacramento becomes the state capital

1869 Transcontinental railroad links California to rest of the U.S.

1871 Anti-Chinese riots break out in San Francisco

1873 Modoc War; last Indian resistance to white settlement in California

American

1492 Christopher Columbus reaches America

1607 Jamestown (Virginia) founded by English colonists

1620 Mayflower arrives at Plymouth (Massachusetts)

1754–63 French and Indian War

1765 Parliament passes Stamp Act

1775–83 Revolutionary War

1776 Signing of the Declaration of Independence

1788–90 First congressional elections

1791 Bill of Rights added to U.S. Constitution

1803 Louisiana Purchase

1812–14 War of 1812

1820 Missouri Compromise

1836 Battle of the Alamo, Texas

1846–48 Mexican-American War

1849 California Gold Rush

1860 South Carolina secedes from Union

1861–65 Civil War

1862 Lincoln signs Homestead Act

1863 Emancipation Proclamation

1865 President Lincoln assassinated (April 14)

1865–77 Reconstruction in the South

1866 Civil Rights bill passed

1881 President James Garfield shot (July 2)

History

1896 First Ford automobile is made

1898–99 Spanish-American War

1901 President William McKinley is shot (Sept. 6)

1917 U.S. enters World War I

1922 Nineteenth Amendment passed, giving women the vote

1929 U.S. stock market crash; Great Depression begins

1933 Franklin D. Roosevelt becomes president; begins New Deal

1941 Japanese attack Pearl Harbor (Dec. 7); U.S. enters World War II

1945 U.S. drops atomic bomb on Hiroshima and Nagasaki; Japan surrenders, ending World War II

1963 President Kennedy assassinated (November 22)

1964 Civil Rights Act passed

1965–73 Vietnam War

1968 Martin Luther King, Jr., shot in Memphis (April 4)

1974 President Richard Nixon resigns because of Watergate scandal

1979–81 Hostage crisis in Iran: 52 Americans held captive for 444 days

1989 End of U.S.-Soviet cold war

1991 Gulf War

1993 U.S. signs North American Free Trade Agreement with Canada and Mexico

California History

1906 Earthquake and fire devastate San Francisco

1911 First movie made in Hollywood

1935 Central Valley irrigation project begins

1937 Golden Gate Bridge, crossing San Francisco Bay, is completed

1942 Forced removal of Japanese Americans begins

1953 Los Angeles native Governor Earl Warren becomes chief justice of the U. S.

1964 Student protests begin at University of California, Berkeley

1965 Race riots in Los Angeles

1968 Redwood National Park opens

• California native Richard Nixon is elected president of the U.S.

1971 American Indian protesters occupy Alcatraz Island

1973 The first African-American mayor of Los Angeles, Tom Bradley, is elected

1980 Former governor Ronald Reagan elected 40th president of the U.S.

1984 Los Angeles hosts the Summer Olympics

1989 San Francisco area struck by earthquake

1992 53 people die as riots sweep Los Angeles

1994 A major earthquake hits Los Angeles

Junípero Serra (1713–84) A monk of the Franciscan Order, Serra founded nine missions along the coast of California.

John Charles Frémont (1813–90) Frémont explored California as an army officer and was one of the first U.S. senators from California.

Leland Stanford (1824–93) Stanford was part of the "Big Four" that built the Central Pacific Railroad. He served as governor (1862–63) and U.S. senator (1885–93). In 1885, he founded Stanford University in honor of his son.

Levi Strauss (1829–1902) The German-born merchant moved from New York to California during the Gold Rush. To meet miners' needs for strong clothing, Strauss and his brothers began making and selling their famous denim trousers in 1874.

Helen Hunt Jackson (1830–85) A writer and reformer, Jackson protested the federal government's policies toward Native Americans in her book, *A Century of Dishonor* (1881), and in a novel, *Ramona* (1884), set among California's Indians.

John Muir (1838–1914) Muir dedicated his life to preserving the natural heritage of California and other regions. He helped persuade Congress to make Yosemite Valley a national park. Muir also founded the Sierra Club.

Hiram Johnson (1866–1945) A popular, reform-minded governor (1911–17), Johnson was elected to the first of many terms in the U.S. Senate in 1917.

Jack London (1876–1916) This San Francisco native wrote forty-three books, including *The Call of the Wild*.

Earl Warren (1891–1974) A native of Los Angeles, Warren served as California's attorney general (1939–43) and governor (1943–53). He was a chief justice of the U.S. from 1953 to 1969.

Walter Elias Disney (1901–66) Walt Disney produced scores of animated and live-action films. In 1955, Disney opened the Disneyland theme park in Anaheim.

Linus Pauling (b. 1901) Pauling taught at several California schools and won two Nobel prizes: for chemistry in 1954 and for peace in 1962.

Earl Warren

Ansel Adams (1902–84) One of the best-known American photographers, Adams took pictures that captured the natural beauty of California and the West.

Jack London

John Steinbeck (1902–68)
This Salinas-born writer won the Pulitzer Prize in 1940 for *The Grapes of Wrath*, a novel describing the plight of migrant workers during the Depression. In 1962, Steinbeck received the Nobel Prize for literature.

Edmund Gerald Brown (b. 1905) Brown served as district attorney for his native San Francisco (1943–50) and later for the state (1950–59) before election to two terms as governor (1959–67). His son, **Edmund Gerald Brown, Jr. (b. 1938)**, served as governor from 1975 to 1983 and made several unsuccessful attempts to win the Democratic presidential nomination.

S. I. (Samuel Ichiye) Hayakawa (1906–92) Born in British Columbia, Hayakawa was both a U.S. senator from California (1977–83) and a famous scholar. He gained nationwide fame by taking a strong stand against student radicalism on college campuses.

Luis Walter Alvarez (b. 1911) This San Francisco-born scientist and educator won a Nobel Prize in 1966 for his work in physics.

Ronald Reagan (b. 1911)
Moving to California in 1937, Reagan became a successful actor. After becoming involved in politics he was elected to two terms as governor (1967–75) and two terms as U.S. president (1980–88).

Richard Milhous Nixon (1913–94) Nixon was elected to Congress from California in 1948 and served as Dwight Eisenhower's vice president (1958–60). He became the first native-born Californian to be elected president (1968) and was reelected in 1972. The Watergate scandal led to his resignation in 1974.

Thomas Bradley (b. 1917)
Joining the Los Angeles Police Department in 1940, Tom Bradley went on to serve six terms (1973–93) as the first African-American mayor of Los Angeles.

Cesar Chavez (1927–93)
Chavez worked tirelessly to improve conditions for farm workers in California. He founded the organization that became the United Farm Workers of America.

Dianne Feinstein (b. 1933)
Feinstein was a member of the

Barbara Boxer

San Francisco board of supervisors before becoming mayor (1978–88). In 1992, she was elected to the U.S. Senate.

Steven Jobs (b. 1955) and **Stephen Wozniak (b. 1951)** In 1975 Jobs and Wozniak built a computer in a garage in Mill Valley. The success of their company, Apple Computer, and the personal computers they developed helped spark a high-tech boom in California's "Silicon Valley."

Barbara Boxer (b. 1940)
Boxer joined the U.S. Senate in 1993. Before 1993, she had been a member of the House of Representatives for ten years. She has worked to cut military spending and to help women and the environment.

RESOURCE GUIDE

Pictures in this volume:

AFL-CIO: 49 (top)

American Airlines: 44

Apple Computer: 51

Archivos de Indias: 12

Bancroft Library/UC Berkeley: 17 (top)

Boxer Senate Offices: 61

California Division of Tourism: 2, 53

California State Historical Society: 39 (top)

California State Library: 56 (seal), 57 (flower, tree)

DC Public Library: 50

Franklin Delano Roosevelt Library: 25 (top)

Library of Congress: 9 (both), 10, 11, 13 (both), 14, 15, 17 (bottom), 18 (bottom), 19, 20, 21, 22, 23, 25 (bottom), 26, 28, 29, 30, 31, 32, 33, 35 (both), 36, 37, 39 (bottom), 40, 41 (both), 45, 48, 56 (flag), 57 (bird), 60 (both)

National Archives: 47 (both)

Private Collection: 18 (top)

Smithsonian Museum: 49 (bottom)

About the author:

Charles A. Wills is a writer, editor, and consultant specializing in American history. He has written, edited, or contributed to more than thirty books, including many volumes in The Millbrook Press's *American Albums from the Collections of the Library of Congress* series. Wills lives in Dutchess County, New York.

Suggested reading:

Carpenter, Allan, *Enchantment of America: California*, Chicago: Childrens Press, 1978

Caughey, J. W., *California: A Remarkable State's Life History,* New York: Prentice Hall, 1970

Dillon, R. H., *Humbugs and Heros: A Gallery of California Pioneers,* Yosemite, 1983

Knill, Harry, *The Story of Early California to 1894,* Santa Barbara, CA: Bellerophon, 1988

Lavender, D. S., *California: A Bicentennial History,* New York: Norton, 1976

Van Steenwyck, Elizabeth, *The California Gold Rush: West with the Forty-niners,* New York: Franklin Watts, 1991

For more information contact:

California Historical Society
2099 Pacific Avenue
San Francisco, CA 94109
Tel. (415) 567-1848

California Office of Tourism
1030 13th Street
Sacramento, CA 95814
Tel. (800) 862-2543

INDEX

Page numbers in *italics* indicate illustrations